LeBron James

Basketball Legend

By Shanya Worthy

Gareth Stevens
Publishing

Please visit our Web site www.garethstevens.com. For a free color catalog of all our high-quality books, call toll free 1-800-542-2595 or fax 1-877-542-2596.

Library of Congress Cataloging-in-Publication Data

Worthy, Shanya.
LeBron James : basketball legend / Shanya Worthy.
    p. cm. — (Inspiring lives)
Includes index.
ISBN 978-1-4339-3638-8 (pbk.)
ISBN 978-1-4339-3639-5 (6-pack)
ISBN 978-1-4339-3637-1 (library binding)
1. James, LeBron—Juvenile literature. 2. Basketball players—United States—Biography—Juvenile literature. I. Title.
GV884.J86W67 2010
796.323092—dc22
[B]
                                        2009037279

Published in 2010 by Gareth Stevens Publishing
111 East 14th Street, Suite 349
New York, NY 10003

Copyright © 2010 Gareth Stevens Publishing

Designer: Michael J. Flynn
Editor: Greg Roza

Photo credits: Cover (LeBron James), title page (LeBron James) © Gregory Shamus/ Getty Images; cover (court), title page (court), pp. 5, 29 © Elsa/Getty Images; p. 7 © Steve Grayson/WireImage/Getty Images; p. 9 © Stephen Dunn/Getty Images; p. 11 © Michael J. LeBrecht II/Sports Illustrated/Getty Images; p. 13 © Greg Nelson/ Sports Illustrated/Getty Images; p. 15 © Tom Pidgeon/Getty Images; pp. 17, 27 © David Liam Kyle/National Basketball Association/Getty Images; p. 19 © Jennifer Pottheiser/ National Basketball Association/Getty Images; p. 21 © Andy Lyons/Getty Images; p. 23 © Streeter Lecka/Getty Images; p. 25 © Jeff Haynes/AFP/Getty Images.

Printed in the United States of America

CPSIA compliance information: Batch #CW10GS: For further information contact Gareth Stevens, New York, New York at 1-800-542-2595.

Contents

Meet LeBron

LeBron James is a pro basketball player.

He plays for the Cleveland Cavaliers.

Growing Up

LeBron was born in 1984. He grew up in Akron, Ohio.

LeBron's mom, Gloria, raised him by herself. She had to work very hard.

Playing Sports

LeBron began playing basketball when he was very young. He practiced running, jumping, and shooting.

LeBron was also very good at football. He was quick and strong.

LeBron played basketball in high school.

His team was called the Fighting Irish.

LeBron helped the Fighting Irish win many games. Basketball fans started calling him "King James."

Going Pro

LeBron joined the NBA in 2003 when he was just 18! The Cleveland Cavaliers picked him for their team.

LeBron has been one of the best players in pro basketball. He was named Rookie of the Year in 2004!

21

LeBron played in the 2008 summer Olympics. He helped the U.S. basketball team win gold medals!

All About LeBron

LeBron wears number 23. His favorite basketball player wore that number. That player's name is Michael Jordan.

Michael Jordan

LeBron has a family. LeBron's family includes his sons, LeBron Jr. and Bryce, and their mother Savannah.

What's Next, LeBron?

LeBron was the NBA Most Valuable Player in 2009! What's next for LeBron James?

1984 LeBron James is born.

1999 LeBron joins the Fighting Irish.

2003 LeBron is picked to join the Cleveland Cavaliers.

2004 LeBron is named the NBA Rookie of the Year.

2008 LeBron helps the U.S. Olympic basketball team win gold medals.

2009 LeBron is named the NBA Most Valuable Player.

For More Information

Books:

Doeden, Matt. *The Best of Pro Basketball.* Mankato, MN:
  Capstone Press, 2010.

Hareas, John. *Baketball.* New York: DK Publishing, 2005.

Jacobs, L. R. *LeBron James: King of the Court.* New York:
  Grosset & Dunlap, 2009.

Tieck, Sarah. *LeBron James: Basketball Superstar.* Edina, MN:
  ABDO Books, 2009.

Web Sites:

LeBron James Biography
www.jockbio.com/Bios/James/James_bio.html

NBA: LeBron James
www.nba.com/playerfile/lebron_james/

Glossary

gold medal: the prize for coming in first in an Olympic event

NBA: the pro basketball league in the United States

Olympics: an event of many sports contests between many countries

pro: someone who gets paid to play a sport

rookie: someone who is new to a job or sports league

valuable: thought highly of because of personal skills

Index